The Secret Not Being Spoken About

Spoken About

Why Activating Your Pineal Gland Is So Important For Sustaining Higher Consciousness

Helen Jane Rose

Website: **www.soulconsciousbeing.com**

CONTENTS

Introduction

1	Honouring The Higher Intelligence Within You	1
2	Breaking Through The Death Trap	9
3	The Shift From Mass To Soul Consciousness	15
4	Service To Self – The Most Important Step To Take	21
5	The Sacredness of Inner Silence - A Key To Pineal Gland Activation	27
6	A Leap In Understanding And Acceptance	35
7	Your Purpose Is About So Much More Than Your Physic Gifts	43
8	Making Peace With Your Energy In Motion	49
9	Joshua Ben Joseph Speaks	57

"The greatest problem for humanity isn't what's happening on the outside – it's what's going on within each individual who has forgotten who they really are. If everyone realised the truth, that they are a soul housed within a body, with the use of a mind that either enhances their experience of themselves or hinders it, life as we know it would change dramatically."

Introduction

Welcome to an unusual book that has come into form through the process of automatic writing. This little book is about the huge importance of activating your Pineal Gland. It's a direct communication from a group of highly evolved beings known as The Enlightened Conscious Collaboration.

This is how we refer to ourselves as The Enlightened Conscious Collaboration and communicate to you through the hand of our scribe. It could also be said that our scribe's higher consciousness is also relaying this information to you. She uses a variation of automatic writing techniques to set aside her thoughts and check into the higher wisdom that flows through her hands. Her hands heal through the words that she brings through from higher consciousness.

We wish for our words to soothe your soul and help you remember some truths that are dormant within you, that are waiting to be activated. The intent of this little book is to assist you in coming home to soul consciousness, to move you away from the mass thought forms that have kept you controlled and locked into a system that we now want to free you from.

Many would read these words and not believe a word that is written here. But for those who have been called through the magnetism of your hearts, you will know truth when it is spoken to you. It will matter not what another conditioned one might say to you, for you will suddenly become aware of a deeper part of yourself that is now ready to be activated.

We are relying on many of you to wake up to your true brilliance, to love yourselves for the amazing souls that you are. To take a stand in whatever way is right for you, so that you can come to fully own your inner peace, freedom and allow your light to shine through.

We aim with this book to start the process of fully activating your Pineal Gland, to restore it to its former glory, as in the days of Atlantis. Since those days it has been unable to connect into soul consciousness in the fully awakened way that it can now. Many of you have gained a state of awakening and enlightenment that is now on a different level to that of before. This is based on the collective consciousness of so many volunteers who are deliberately here at this time to hold the vibration of Soul Consciousness/I AM Presence to ensure the Divine Plan of creating The New Earth. To support the return to abundance, joy, co-operation, compassion and unconditional love of self and others.

A great change in the overall consciousness of the planet is taking place, but the shift needs to be spearheaded by the ones who are being called upon now, who will not bend to the mass consciousness and fear that is to override everything. You have all placed yourselves in the perfect positions to rise from the ashes of fear and self-doubt, to return to and fully embody the divine beings that you are. A cliché yes but it is your time to shine.

Your path was different to many around you. Past lessons haven't been your building blocks so to speak. It has always been about you developing your inner skills to have an outer impact on the world. Through your meditations, healings, workshops and reading you have brought yourselves to an evolved position that now calls for your return to full soul consciousness and the great benefits that brings you. It's the call away from mass consciousness. It's the call to finally, fully come home to your divinity and the celebration that brings. It brings with it a soul celebration, where you move from karma to dharma, from acting for soul growth to being a catalyst for others evolution into soul consciousness.

The path where you are headed will offer you a lightness of being that you have not yet experienced in this lifetime. You are headed for en-lighten-ment - the most joyful place a human being could ever be.

You might find that some of the text housed within this book is strong, could be viewed as judgmental and might provoke some inner resistance from within you. This is its exact aim. Some parts are deliberately included to provoke and bring out inner beliefs to be transformed and transmuted. We hope you enjoy the inner changes that this book will gift you,

We are The Enlightened Conscious Collaboration,

Peace Is Within You.

Helen Jane Rose

1

Honouring The Higher Intelligence Within You

"Here in lies the secret to the survival of the species. It rests in the recognition that it's from the being that the doing should emerge."

1

The keys to the codes of Pineal Gland Activation can be found within this text. This book was formed through a new technology, Soul Consciousness Technology, which is yet to be understood on the planet. In future books we will be talking in greater detail about this new technology that's now being released. It has great power to transform. It is technology being used for the betterment of humanity, rather than against it.

How technology is used by a planet is the key to the planet's spiritual maturity. It is coming to a time when those using technology against the masses must be called into account. For technology should be used to advance a civilization for the good of the whole - not to financially benefit the good of a few.

We cannot change anything from afar, as this goes against the Universal Codes of Conduct. So we are now upping the game so to speak, in encouraging those powerhouses of light to shine the truth into the darkest parts of humanity, to help bring awareness to how the planet has been manipulated. It is time for exposures on an unprecedented scale, in order to change the overall consciousness, which will then literally change the world. For thoughts affect every action that is taken on the planet. And the controllers can only control whilst the consciousness is ignorant to what is really going on. For ignorance is not bliss. Living separated from the true self will never make anyone happy. Inner happiness can only happen when you are united with the truth of who you really are.

The Pineal Gland has literally been attacked by technology being used against you to keep you from remembering who you really are. It is time for the technology that will reverse this to be released to you. Enough have consciously asked for this to be so, as more and more of humanity demands their freedom. Mind control can only last whilst the overall consciousness demands it. In other words mind control can only be effective whilst the majority of humanity are happy to be controlled by their minds. As people start to realise the truth that they are slaves to their minds, so global mind control will cease to exist.

It is only through the deep belief that the mind has authority over you that the planet has been able to get into the mess that it is in. Too much adoration has been placed on the mind. Let us go one step further than has perhaps been currently touched upon by your civilization. History reminds us of the futility of bowing to material objects. The Old Testament referred to this as bowing to false gods. Now the majority of humanity is bowing to the most negative false god of them all - their minds. They are idolizing the part of themselves that keeps them trapped in judgement, disharmony, disunity and most of all trapped in the past.

You see your mind, however clever it has been made out to be, cannot reside in the present moment, for that is the divine time and space of your soul. Your mind only knows the past, and denies the truth that you are a soul. Therefore it convinces you that it knows best and that it is perfectly sensible for you to live from the past. Your mind then projects your past onto your future. By this we mean that the mind has no way of understanding the deeper purpose of your life, so it lives in fear of the future. This is where worry, anxiety and stress come from. If the mind didn't worry about what was going to occur you would not suffer from worry and stress. This is why the mindfulness revolution has become so prevalent on the planet, reminding the rich West that they are missing a very important piece of the puzzle. They may be exceeding the rest of the world in material gain yet their souls are devoid of any nurture.

The soul's expression has been cut off by the illusions of the mind and is being ignored, unable to express itself. When in reality the mind should be honouring the soul. This you might say is because the planet has forgotten that they are divine beings, housing the God consciousness within themselves.

~

The soul brings life into what would otherwise be lifeless. It is very hard to read these words and really assimilate them, as so much focus of society is on the body. Yes your body is your temple but not for the reasons that have been propagated. Your body is your temple because it holds your treasure – the real you – your soul. A body cannot exist without a soul – it is null and void without it. When it is no longer required by the soul, the body is ritually buried in a box in the ground or turned to dust through cremation. This is in no way supposed to sound morbid, it is the truth of what happens when the soul leaves the body and no longer requires or needs a physical experience.

Your soul stays present within your body through your breath. It is the mechanism of your breath that keeps your body working so that it can house your soul. Your soul controls your body – not the other way around. The mind thinks it is controlling your body but this simply isn't true. Your soul is communicating to your body every second of the day.

Just think for a moment – your mind has no control over your breath. You do not tell your body to breathe, when to and how to – it happens outside of your mind's abilities. You cannot explain how this happens, only that it does. Of course you can become mindful of your breathing and as such bring a new awareness to your breath (a sacred spiritual practice) yet your breath is controlled by intelligence beyond your mind. It is the same intelligence that keeps nature alive, to nurture you. It is the higher consciousness that is responsible for the creation of life itself. Man can create things, but nature can only be created by the universal consciousness that is so far beyond the intelligence of the mind.

~

Your soul's purpose is to guide you back to eventually

realising who you really are. It is no more complicated and so much more profound than many could possibly realise. When you finally become aware that you are your soul and not your body, so the communication no longer needs to feed through your body. You merge with your true self and feel its guidance in every second of the day through being present to it in each moment of each day.

Your soul is the one powering your body, yet it's being completely neglected and ignored by most on the planet. But this isn't written in judgement, as from a higher perspective it was meant to be this way. However this is changing, as the evolution of consciousness takes its place on the main stage of humanity's development. Humanity must now remember that its primary purpose for being here is for the journey of the soul. This is the purpose of coming into a body. The purpose is not to amass as much wealth as possible. This is not so. However, by honouring your soul you automatically bring wealth to you – inner and outer wealth. Money is a holy and divine currency when it is used for the betterment of yourself and your civilization.

The purpose of the journey is to truly become a human 'being'. To remember the spiritual being that you really are. To remember the divine presence that has been hidden from your conscious awareness. To accept you have believed the propaganda that you are just your body. The idea is for you to awaken to the reality that your joy, peace and true fulfillment in this lifetime, rests on you living in the present, being in the now of each moment. It is living in divine time and fully accepting that each moment is exactly as it is supposed to be.

Please note that the human race is not called human 'doings'. And here in lies the secret to the survival of the species. It rests in the recognition that it's from the being that the doing should emerge.

2

Breaking Through The Death Trap

"Competition will soon lead to co-operation on an unpreceded scale. Competition will be seen as such an outdated concept that the civilization that believed in its truth will look back and realise its futility."

2

Everyone is living in denial of who they really are, and whilst it seems convenient at the moment not to try and understand this truth, in time it will be absolutely necessary. For every aspect of the human drama has an opposite. Why yearn and strive so strongly for material gain, when you will have the dilemma of having to let it all go when you are ready to leave. Isn't it the fool that puts all his time and effort into amassing, forgetting that he is supposed to be living, and then everything he has put his time and effort into he is forced by nature to leave behind. Those tortuous last years send shock waves across the planetary conscious grid creating more and more fear. Please take a moment to digest this fact. Everyone's thoughts have an impact on everyone else. The more poignant the thought the bigger the impact.

It is a fact that someone who has amassed so much material gain and solely identifies with it, will experience much more suffering on the realisation that they will have to let it all go, and therefore their identity, than someone who has lived a so called 'poor' life but has been focused on being of help and service to others. Neither are healthy positions for a human being to be in yet the latter, which is looked down upon by society is actually far more beneficial to you personally than the former. You have been taught to honour false gods who do not know themselves and live in fear every day of not being the best. We wish for what we say not to sound judgemental, what we are attempting to do is activate higher consciousness within you.

If you are one of the multi-millionaires who will be reading this text please read the next few paragraphs with an open mind and openness for self-inquiry. Your soul is calling you to contemplate the following fact. You are being called to use your genius at creating to help humanity now – to move from self-interest to assisting the greater plan. However harsh this might sound it is true – if you have not invested any of your time into helping humanity and only taking from them, you will reach a point of terror when you come close to so called death. This is a fact, this is truth. For the closer you get to passing, the closer you get to your soul and the realisation of who you really are.

Will your legacy be that you left multi-million pound houses to your family and a business that convinced a gullible public that your product could help them? Did you make your money by persuading people through manipulation that what you could offer them would help them? Maybe you truly believed in your business and that it was helping people, but what have you really done other than spend your entire life on the self-interest of you and your family? If you have only supported yourself and your family please do not kid yourselves - you have really only supported yourselves. For supporting your families is part of your ego need. Of course it is noble to look after your family, but we assure you that you will come to the point of feeling most terrible that you did not do what you could to help humanity. Until those last years it would have never been a thought, but in those final it is all consuming.

Competition will soon lead to co-operation on an unpreceded scale. Competition will be seen as such an outdated concept that the civilization that believed in its truth will look back and realise its futility. There is no such thing as competition, even though your minds have convinced you that there is. There can't be because at a deeper level you are all one in consciousness. You worry about people taking ideas from you – but where do the ideas come from? Your mind can only think in the past – so where do new ideas come from? They come from your soul – they come from the real you that is connected to the creator (God if you like). Every new creation has come about this way. Can people steal your ideas? Well of course they can – but you have a flow of universal creative energy at your finger-tips. So if someone decides that your idea is so grand that they want to copy it – you have the ability to create a grander version. Is that competition or just trying to bring into form a better version of something you originally created? What you should be worrying about more than competition is considering if your creation is helping or harming the planet? Is what you are creating causing karma or dharma? If it is causing karma then ask yourself why? Why would you want to create something that will cause you strife as a result of it, and everyone else too? The answer is you cannot ask yourself these questions if you do not believe that you are a soul here in a human body. That's the crux of it and what is learnt at the instance of what is known as death.

Death in reality is simply the time the soul leaves the body – its work is completed in physical form. The perception in time to come will be a celebration of the life, whose purpose all along was to come to know itself as its soul.

3

The Shift From Mass To Soul Consciousness

"It is metaphorically the story of the caterpillar that blossoms into the butterfly. Your wings were clipped but now you are being asked to fly - by shedding all that no longer serves you. The caterpillar was always a butterfly, it just didn't see itself as such."

3

When the Pineal Gland is fully activated it forms a smooth shape – the complete opposite to its traditional pine cone form that has always been associated with the gland. It is no coincidence that a statue of a pine cone can be seen in the grounds of the Vatican and many other places on earth. Many believe that they have successfully taken complete hostage of this control centre of the human body, but they are mistaken. When one awakens to the calling of their soul they move into the transcendence stages of moving beyond identifying with mass conscious thought forms. Like attracts like, and like a magnet pulling towards itself its own reflection, so the soon to be enlightened one calls everything to them through the magnetism of their heart yearnings. Pineal Gland Activation happens as a consequence of such an inner transformation. For many their soul guides them to sources who can help them to facilitate such a growth in remembering and consciousness. If you were drawn to this little book then your soul has sought you to be here in this moment receiving these pockets of Soul Conscious Technology, that will have the most lasting and life transforming effects on you.

Everything that you are drawing to yourself is for the purpose of bringing you back to who you truly are.

As you start to realise the eternal truth that you are so much more than you ever imagined yourself to be, so the qualities that you have been desperately searching for such as inner peace, real self-esteem, confidence, self-love (the divine qualities that are dormant in most) get activated once again and you realise how important you really are. But not from an ego point of view, from your soul perception. It is metaphorically the story of the caterpillar that blossoms into the butterfly. Your wings were clipped but now you are being asked to fly - by shedding all that no longer serves you. The caterpillar was always a butterfly, it just didn't see itself as such. Through its transformation and transmutation of all that it wasn't it comes to see itself for all that it really is.

The truth is, and as science will prove, when the Pineal Gland is activated to only receive soul consciousness it forms a round formation much like a light bulb. For all enlightened folk this is how the Pineal Gland looks within the body – just like a light bulb. It glows within the head and its external manifestation is that of a holy halo. You have seen this image around the enlightened one known as Jesus, in beautiful portraits and it is quite true. The artists had soul sight and could see the external manifestation of the activated Pineal Gland as a halo around the head of the master of human consciousness.

Basically it really is quite simple. All enlightened ones, who have throughout history been put on a pedestal are the same as you – they just remembered so and acted so and so their lives took on the miraculous. That is what is being offered to you too. For you would not be reading these words and have an interest in activating your Pineal Gland if the deeper you wasn't calling you to remember who you truly are. You are the master that you have been waiting for. You are your own saviour. This is what Jesus taught and what we are teaching and reminding you of now.

Our aim is to activate in you this truth so that you can leave behind societal and family conditioning and return home to the true you. It is time for you to remember the shining bright light that you are and bring your soul gifts to a world that desperately needs you. But more importantly than what you can offer the world, is what you can offer yourself. And that is coming to know the truth, and allowing yourself to shine.

4

Service To Self - The Most Important Step To Take

"We are here to pull you away from mass conscious thought forms and remind you that what you really want is to be the self-expression of who you really are."

4

Stop hiding. Enough is enough. The small you has had enough too or you wouldn't be reading these words. Just by the fact that you have been drawn to this book means that you are ready to embrace, integrate and make reality your purpose for being here. We want to reiterate again. Your purpose first and foremost is service to self.

Before you can offer unconditional love to anyone else on the planet you must offer it to yourself first. We want you to be of service in the complete opposite way to that which your society and mass consciousness has suggested that you should be. We want you to honour you first and foremost, be selfish if you like, be very selfish and out of that selfishness you will thrive, for you will be honouring you. And honouring you is the most holy place you can be.

You have been conditioned to believe that giving yourself to others is holy, is righteous, but we tell you this is an illusion created by a society based on materialism, based on honouring false gods. To honour the true god within you, you must first serve yourself. You must look honestly at your life and make the decision about what in your life is holding you back from the joy that you should be feeling. We can help you with this, even if you cannot see it. You are being held back by all the people around you. This isn't a judgement, merely a fact. They have played their roles perfectly in getting you to this point, but if you truly want to honour yourself and thrive you will have to let them go - not physically but emotionally. You are putting too much energy and emotion into what they want from you, at the expense of what you want for you. We are here to pull you away from mass conscious thought forms and remind you that what you really want is to be the self-expression of who you really are. An infinite wise being and consciousness who agreed to come to earth at this time to help with the awakening of society. To move humanity forward from a place of stuck servitude to becoming the creator beings that you truly are.

It was never going to be easy. You agreed to your mission but signed on the dotted line to forget it once you were born. You would have moments throughout your life of knowing you were here for a bigger purpose, of wanting to talk about the big stuff when all those around you were sweating the small things, but you couldn't grasp why you felt different. Then a life changing event woke you up and you could never be conditioned again. You agreed to the time, place and event that would be the catalyst to awakening to your true self and waking up from the dream, and learning and remembering about reality. We can tell you that your true awakening happened around the earth year of 2009. Before that you were preparing but when you started to fully awaken to Soul, Source, God Consciousness was during that year. It was the same for everyone despite how many years you have been on the spiritual path. You set traps along the way to really make you desire enlightenment, for you are too wise not to know the laws of the universe.

What we want to make clear is that despite many of you believing in your low self-worth stories you are all highly evolved beings. As Neale Donald Walsh would say you are HEBs! All who are reading this are so evolved that we are in awe of your tenacity and agreement to go into a planet that is so behind, so immature and still find your spiritual maturity and truth amongst a populace who deems you insane. But they are the insane ones believing that they are just human – that life resolves solely around them and that when they die that's it. It's insanity at its best yet they have convinced you that they are right.

We must say for the benefit of you coming into your Soul Consciousness they are wrong. Completely and utterly wrong. They couldn't be further from the truth. But they are here to learn different lessons to you. You who are reading this text without contempt but with an open heart, are here to remember, not learn. You have learnt all the lessons - you are simply remembering. And we are making a clarion call, through our faithful scribe to you, calling you to wake up to the reality of who you are. You are the ascended masters, spiritual masters, thought leaders of all ages, the saints and the sages – you are all brothers and sisters. You are all unique but one at the same time, and you made a pact. To serve yourselves first, through inner guidance and then to serve humanity. You knew that at the right time you would all come together through synchronicity, through the universal law of like attracts like, and all play your parts in The Divine Plan. That time is nigh and we are counting on one million to hear our call and jump into action.

All your purposes are different but united. You are all here to uniquely remind the human populace that they are here for a reason. That there is nothing haphazard and chaotic about their life. That it was chosen perfectly for the lessons that they are here to learn.

5

The Sacredness of Inner Silence - A Key To Pineal Gland Activation

"You will understand that it is your right to live and breathe the expression of your soul, using your higher intelligence to navigate you on earth, moment to moment."

5

As your Pineal Gland activates more fully, you will start to question things that before you had not thought to. Take for example the British Monarchy – you will look at the situation as ridiculous that certain souls claim to be more important and expect servitude from the rest. You will see clearly that the entire system has been set up to honour false gods at the expense of yourselves. But again there is nothing to fear, as it was all set up this way within The Divine Plan. As you further activate your Pineal Gland and move more deeply into higher consciousness you will start to see the illusion more clearly. You will understand that it is your right to live and breathe the expression of your soul, using your higher intelligence to navigate you on earth, moment to moment. Some might deem you crazy – yet others would see you as free.

You start to free yourself as soon as you realise that it is possible to. That you can live in the now, moment to moment in unison with your soul's guidance, just like the way it navigates your breath allowing you to continue to live, without having to consciously think how to. Stop for a moment. Please take a deep breath. Please set your intention to now receive the energetic codes that are going to be activated from within you. You knew that at this very moment you would call yourself here to receive the codes to lift you to your next evolutionary leap in consciousness; to become more self-assured of the brilliant light that is alive within you. To step more fully away from fear and into your next level of unconditional love for yourself first and then for all others.

Wherever and whenever you put your attention onto anything you activate a response from the universe. This exercise is set in motion to start a universal response to your deeper awakening. This activation is not bound by time and space – it works in the here and now. All Soul Conscious Technology works this way.

~

Breathe in slowly and breathe out. Bring your attention to your breath. Keep breathing in and out – do this four times consciously. Feel yourself starting to relax. Now breathe in through your nose and imagine that the air you are breathing in is really thousands of energetic particles coming into your body and moving down into your stomach. Keep breathing in and out. Feel a peace in your body as you do this focusing more on breathing in than on breathing out. Try and put all of your attention on breathing into your stomach. Make your breath in longer than your breaths out. Breathe in for the count of four and out for the count of one. Breath in through your nose and out through your mouth. Hear yourself pushing your breath out in a quick movement. Do this six times. Feel your stomach respond to your conscious breaths. Imagine your stomach starting to light up as it's receiving the energetic codes that are birthing in you. Visualize bright light in your stomach. Sit with this image for a few moments. Imagine coming from your stomach millions of pathways dispersing the energetic light to every corner of your body - focus on this now. See your whole body being filled with light coming from your stomach. See the light moving down to the tips of your toes, through your arms to your fingertips and up your spine to the top of your head. Bring your attention back to your stomach and see that it's still lit up with bright white energetic particles of light. Now move your attention to a light within the middle of your forehead. Visualize a white rod of light going from the light in your stomach to the light in middle of your forehead. Sit and focus on this light. Put all of your attention on the light in the middle of your head. Hold your attention there. As you do this you will start to visualize rods of light coming from every side of the light in the middle of your head - they will look like spokes. If you cannot sense or see these rods start to visualize them now. However you see them is perfect exactly as they appear to you – everyone will have a unique and individual experience. Sit with this experience for a few moments and then visualize the rod of light moving down through your body through your stomach, to the base of your spine and then splitting and going down your legs and out your feet and moving deep into the earth. Sit feeling completely connected to the earth for a few moments. Now feel energy from the earth move back up through your feet and rest in your stomach. Know that you have now grounded yourself and set your activation in motion. Sit for a little while longer enjoying the peace that you will now feel.

Congratulations you have just received a Pineal Gland Activation through Soul Conscious Technology. The energetic codes that have been downloaded to you will start to work with your mind, sending neurological pathways throughout the cells of your body. These cells are carrying new awareness, garnered from the activation. The activation also wakes up sleeping cells that are ready to awaken to your new reality. Your body has been automatically sent signals to allow in the flow of Soul Consciousness and to start to physically block the effect of receiving mass conscious signals. They go through the pathway of the third eye and are filtered by the Pineal Gland as now acceptable to pass on to the body and transmit - moving you to start to experience more inner peace, helping you to recognise the silence within yourself. We have assisted in shutting down the receptors that feed off of the all-consuming dramas of everyday life, to allow for a new level of consciousness to enter through the sacred eye.

In time and as your consciousness heightens no one will ever be able to control your thought patterns again – and you will start to become fashioned to use thought as a creative means of achieving the life of your dreams, instead of a life lived from fear. You will start to remember who you really are.

Being fully present in the moment means to fully merge with your soul and the source of all-that-is. It is through the silence that the miracle of transcendence occurs. It is through the realization that your soul has been waiting for your recognition all along, your realization that you are already everything that you longed for yourself to be. From the higher conscious perspective you are overcoming the biggest challenge that any human could ever expect to find themselves in – moving from the dream into reality.

Please do not worry if you found the instructions for the Pineal Gland Activation hard to follow. A more in-depth audio version of the activation is offered here www.soulconsciousbeing.com/pineal-gland-activation/ and is highly recommended. The benefit of this audio is that you receive the frequencies in a more direct and powerful way, as our scribes voice is used to transfer codes directly to you. It's suggested that you listen to the audio every day for 21 days to get the maximum benefit, however it is also advisable to follow your own intuition as to the frequency of its use.

THE SECRET NOT BEING SPOKEN ABOUT

6

A Leap In Understanding And Acceptance

"It's this knowing, this longing for things to be different that sets you apart from the rest of humanity. You know in the depth of your being that there's another way to live."

6

Quite simply the year 2016 was deemed by the universe as the time of universal change. It was deemed and planned to be the year when one million would finally wake up to the truth of who they really are. They would realise that their past was simply a stepping stone to becoming fully conscious, and like the butterfly that sheds it cocoon they would let go of everything that no longer served them. They would find peace with the truth that whatever unkindness they had endured they volunteered to; that they agreed to transmute and transcend the pain in their service to The Divine Plan.

A shift in consciousness sees you knowing that you were never the victim of anything that happened to you. That you agreed to transmute collective pain - what a selfless thing to do! Seen from this perspective you are powerful beyond measure. You also knew that to be a leader in manifesting all that you wanted to, to live the life of your dreams, you had to know its contrast or you had nothing to compare it to. A cliché yes but you cannot truly know the heights of joy if you have not experienced the depths of despair. The light only knows itself within the contrast of darkness. This is the game of duality on planet earth, and in making peace with this reality you free yourself from the grip of your mind.

You also agreed to become the biggest

empathizer it was possible to be. That compassion and unconditional love would be the crux of how your life would be run. To experience all that you are not, so as to become all that you really are. To be a beacon of light, a bridge if you like to bring others back to themselves too. It's no mean feat to break through! You agreed to act as a bridge to help others move from surviving to thriving, inner chaos to inner peace to becoming the bright shining light that you are destined to be.

So love the ones who caused you so much strife for they are trapped within a prison confined by walls of guilt. It might not be obvious on the surface but inside they are in turmoil. Without your consent at a very deep level they couldn't have acted towards you how they did. Yes this is controversial but it is universal truth. You are all creator beings. But where creation differs is that all who are reading this book volunteered to undergo abusive situations to heal them on behalf of humanity. You all agreed to be born into abusive genealogy, to extended family trees dating back thousands of years of a hidden history of abuse. This abuse will have manifested in the form of mental, emotional, physical or sexual abuse. Controlling relationships are forms of mental abuse. Unless someone consciously comes to this realisation and sees this and transmutes the energy of abuse it will never leave the planet. There isn't a saviour as your religions have tried to convey, who sweeps down and clears all mankind's misdemeanours. No it is only through mankind evolving that changes can take place.

In the Age of Empowerment it is about taking personal responsibility for healing the past and stepping into co-creating the future.

As the past is fully healed from within you, you come to the grander realisation. That those that hurt you were playing their part to enable you to experience all that you were not - in helping you find your divinity amongst a planet that had collectively deemed it impossible to. The Universe/Source/The-All-That-Is loves everyone unconditionally, without any judgement as this is impossible to, for it is through the human mind that judgements occur. For from the higher planes of consciousness and where we are leading you there is no right and wrong or good and bad. The mind cannot comprehend these truths, yet the activated heart knows they are true.

As your consciousness expands so does the peace within you, as you move away from fear and fully embody the divine frequency of unconditional love. Set your intention now to move more fully from your mind into your heart - make loving yourself unconditionally your goal. Accept all that you are, embrace everything.

There are approximately one million of you who agreed to this adventure – who agreed that you would forget who you were, but feel at a deep level that you didn't fit in and that you were here to serve; yourselves first and then the greater plan. This feeling of being a square peg in a round hole would eventually lead you to the thought and feeling 'enough is enough'. And on saying this to yourselves with the deep meaning and purpose behind it, the universal door of freedom would open. You would be pushed to the point where even the most asleep of you would cry from the roof tops, scream from the top of your lungs: "Enough is enough". It's this knowing, this longing for things to be different that sets you apart from the rest of humanity. You know in the depth of your being that there's another way to live, and deny it all you like it catches up with you in that moment of spiritual awakening when you claim: "Enough is enough". All spiritual masters in the past have reached this point. It is the creative bridge for leaving the old world and entering the new.

The New Earth offers miracles that you cannot comprehend because the culture and society of the old world cannot believe it to be true. They are only privy to a world steeped in fear, that lacks unconditional love, where the fittest and the most selfish thrive. You are here to leave this world behind. You are here to enter the kingdom of heaven. You are here to thrive and show those that know no different that there is an alternative way to live. You are here to show the world who you really are - from all your vulnerabilities to your divine amazingness.

You all possess at least two divine gifts that are waiting to birth in you. This may be clairvoyance, clairsentience, aura specialists, energy healers, planetary healers, consciousness caretakers, keepers of wisdom, Ashkaic Record keepers and so many more roles that lots of books could be written on this subject alone. You all have unique roles yet you all have a common purpose – to love yourselves first and foremost for the amazing highly evolved souls that you are, and with that love fully living through every cell in your body, leave your unique mark on the world. All your purposes are needed now and it's up to all of you to unravel them.

7

Your Purpose Is About So Much More Than Your Physic Gifts

"As your consciousness rises due to your spiritual growth, so your Pineal Gland moves to its next stage of en-lighten-ment. The more light it can hold and vibrate, the more you will feel joy from the depth of your being."

7

Activating your third eye or more truthfully your Pineal Gland isn't a complicated job, and shouldn't be used purely for the intention of awakening physic gifts as has popularly been suggested. For true happiness, joy and living on purpose and with passion the gifts need to come as a consequence of the drive for inner peace. If you get stuck on developing the physic gifts at the expense of your own soul evolution the gifts will become a curse because you will not see the bigger picture.

Anyone can open to their physic gifts, for everyone is spiritual and has these gifts waiting dormant to be ignited from within them. But what only the few can do is awaken to their true divine selves, full of compassion, love and higher wisdom that goes way beyond the gifts as such. We hope this makes sense that we are drawing you to a much deeper realisation – self-realisation.

Of course your spiritual gifts are important to your purpose but they must not become the driving force otherwise they become a trap. They will trap you without you even realising it. But again nothing happens by accident so even if this be the case it will be the right lesson to learn. However this book is a call to those who are here to remember, not so much to learn. Yes to some extent you are all here to learn but many of you need to remember who you really are – this is the real definition of enlightenment. Remembering and embodying the truth of the 'light' that you are. A magnificent powerful creator being – a holy soul who is waiting to shine through and light up the world. But you have had to experience much darkness to really know the depth of your light. Without the dark you couldn't find the light. This is a spiritual truth as all life on earth is garnered by the experience. You cannot know something unless you have had direct experience of it. Your direct experience of darkness is your springboard to your direct experience of pure light. In a sense the darker the experiences the more extreme the light will be. There's the juxtaposition. Some who have experienced perhaps what we would call the worst extremities of life on earth also have the potential to experience the best.

Inner peace is the prerequisite for the life of pure joy, happiness and passion. Inner peace is where a fully activated Pineal Gland takes you – away from mass consciousness full of fear and survival into the consciousness of the soul. This is when you will thrive – when you are fully aligned with your soul and this is where we want to take you. Just through reading this book and believing what is written here you will start to fully activate your Pineal Gland. You will have moments in meditation of seeing etheric rods coming out of the sides of your head. They will glow a golden hue and you will start to notice them. Sometimes long, short or having disappeared altogether. But over time they will expand and a circle will start to show itself to you. There are some with heightened sight that can see this. Just like there are some who can see auras. This is the aura perfected if you like, as a fully awakened Pineal Gland affects all the rest of the energy systems in the body - from the top down.

We know who each and every one of you are who are reading this book and consciously choosing to activate your Pineal Gland. It is an inner calling to enlightenment. As you consciously focus on this gland it starts to pulse responding to the inner and outer call. It says yes – I hear you – I am ready to work for you at a completely new frequency. The frequency of activation is linked to your consciousness. As your consciousness rises due to your spiritual growth so your Pineal Gland moves to its next stage of en-lighten-ment. The more light it can hold and vibrate the more you will feel joy from the depth of your being.

8

Making Peace With Your Energy In Motion

"All negativity in the world is the outward manifestation of inner chaos...most are at war with themselves rather than at peace and this emulates out and affects everyone."

8

We are most excited that you are here. You will find with an inquiring eye that the Pineal Gland is revered in places that you would find most unexpected. You see there are many in power on the planet who know very well the potential of this illusive gland that doctors and scientists alike claim not to understand. But with the evolution of consciousness taking place on the planet at this time they will soon understand perfectly well that the Pineal Gland cannot be understood from the perception of the mind. It's a bit like Einstein understanding the theory of relativity – he had to reach out of mass consciousness into higher consciousness to bring back this information for humanity to benefit from. And so this is what is being offered to you now.

The benefits of a fully activated Pineal Gland cannot be underestimated. Many in power understand this point perfectly for they have deliberately wanted you to stay ignorant of this fact. But it is time for this information to be accessible to all those who are called to it. For times are a changing and as each and every one of you heal from within so you are having the most incredible effect on the overall consciousness and therefore the planet. For everything is about consciousness. Nothing can really change – no sustainable changes can occur and be held as truth unless the overall consciousness of the planet rises. This is spiritual truth. All negativity in the world is the outward manifestation of inner chaos. The real battles that are going on are those of the mind. Most are at war with themselves rather than at peace and this emulates out and affects everyone. Inner peace starts with inner determination. Positive thinking leads to inner peace. But not in the fake way, where you are covering over negative feelings. All negativity must be healed before real positive thinking can take effect. Those trying to passively think positively without doing the work to release the stuck emotion within themselves are fooling themselves and will feel let down. But they have been let down by not being told the truth that changes everything. Positive thinking can only be effective if you step out of denial and admit that much of how you feel isn't positive.

Negative self talk is the biggest disease on the planet. It causes more self-harm than anything else, yet it can be overcome. It becomes counteracted by honestly looking at your feelings and not denying them. Everyone has a shadow self that needs to be embraced, loved and accepted. It is perfectly natural to feel anger, even hatred towards a situation and the people in it. For often you are feeling like a victim and therefore blame has to be placed. For blame to be placed feelings of a negative nature have to be present. Unless you have completely moved out of victim consciousness you will have negativity running its programming within you. This must be cleared before positive thinking can have the desired effect. One of the most positive things you can think is 'I love myself' - most dislike themselves. If this is true for you please say, at least five times a day – "I love myself" - and fake it until it will become true.

The best advice we can give you on the pathway to inner peace and happiness (and a fully activated Pineal Gland) is start to be honest with yourself. Do not feel ashamed about having thoughts and feelings that aren't deemed 'holy'. You cannot know light if you do not know darkness. You have no marker for inner peace if you have not experienced inner chaos. To know the experience of inner silence is to have known inner noise.

~

Your feelings are your soul speaking to you. How you feel affects how you think and vice versa. If you can open to let your true feelings through, your thinking will change – that we guarantee. For your feelings are your soul calling you to awaken to its presence within you. It's gentle guidance is trying to get your conscious attention. And at the perfect time it will. Not a minute too late, a second too soon. For all is in divine timing. From the higher perspective all is occurring in multi-dimensions. You can jump at any time from one dimension to another – it just takes conscious awareness to do so.

You have a human right to honour how you are feeling – but it's also your right to heal from your hurts – all of them. A change in perception is what is needed. A dose of spiritual unconditional love heals all. This isn't smoochy soft talk this is the science of the universe. Unconditional love is the most potent element in the universe – it can cause instant miracles, it can create instant beauty – it can convert in a nanosecond war into peace. All is possible if you believe it is. You are the only ones stopping yourselves from experiencing the miracles that are your divine birth right to claim.

And so we bring your attention back to the Pineal Gland and its importance for you. Within your glorious body you have all the answers that you need. Each part of your body speaks to you on a daily basis. If you learnt to tune into the language of your body you would know this to be true – as millions do. Your body holds all of your secrets. It is the portal to your soul. In going high sometimes is misunderstood the importance of going within. The problem with going within means facing yourself – all the gory shadow parts, as well as all the glowing.

We are leading you to help yourself in awakening and activating your Pineal Gland by doing some inner spring cleaning. An inner spring clean is needed on a global scale to really start to change the consciousness of the planet. But for now we want to focus on you who have been drawn to read this book. Do not doubt for one second that this book has not called you. For it has. It is calling you, beckoning you to believe its truth, to free you. You are standing on the edge of an evolutionary milestone in the history of the planet – and your planet needs you. But we want you to focus on you before you focus on how you will be of service to the bigger picture. For you wouldn't be reading these words unless you had a purpose that includes service to The Divine Plan. The Divine Plan is talked about in whispers – spoken silently from teacher to student – discussed through word of mouth but nowhere is it written down. For if it was it could be thwarted – and that is not part of the evolution of planet earth. It is a secret plan – known by many yet protected by all in the higher realms. Its secrets cannot be revealed. Call it a sacred text if you like. It cannot be found anywhere. Some have tried through the Akashic Records but it is not possible for it to be accessed from there. It is held in a place that is sacred, that cannot be infiltrated. For that would thwart the beauty of what is to occur. Fear will be rife but not for those who are being called to heal and then stand as stewards for those rising. The spiritual revolution – the rising of the overall consciousness is a given despite what appears to be so much confusion on earth.

9

Joshua Ben Joseph Speaks

"It's the complete letting go of the past, full acceptance of the present and release of the illusion of the future. Time in enlightened consciousness is now."

9

I am Joshua Ben Joseph and I want to talk directly to you about the shift that is occurring that I am partly responsible for, along with so many others. Our job is to ensure that the next stage of evolution takes place on planet earth. My name has been heralded as Jesus Christ, but mostly my messages have been manipulated and totally misunderstood for what I came to do. I came to be the living example of one who is enlightened. Who knows themselves to be that which is not of the human form. To know that underneath the form of the body and the identity of the man, women or child is buried the treasure – their soul, their I Am Presence. Their presence as a part of the god-self of all other humans on earth - the uniting factor between all man. The form is the foothold for the true self but it is in no way the truth of the true self. It is the vehicle to enable the true self to shine through. But it cannot do so whilst you are unconscious and living in the illusion that you are your body and mind. No you are a soul/spiritual being and you entered your body at the perfect time to complete the perfect path that was laid out to you before you incarnated.

We are now calling on those whose job it is to realise that they are the being within their body. That the illusion that they are their mind must be understood to live the holy reality of being one with Source/God. What this means for the planet is profound. Without your self-realisation the species of human beings will cease to exist, based on the very fact that humans aren't being they are doing. So much so that they have prioritized doing over ever needing to be. Therefore they cannot survive for too much longer in the doing, for it has led to the planet being in a mess that cannot be comprehended from most people's living rooms. It's easy to stay blinkered when there is no real way of knowing how much bludgeoning is going on in the world. Millions are being killed every day and the world is oblivious to it. This is not said in judgement. It is said for the need for so many to wake up to the reality that the external is merely a reflection of the internal. Whilst the majority of humanity rests in internal chaos the outer manifestations have to be so. But once a certain amount of the population are living in internal peace then the outer reflection of the world will be a very different one. The one that is often referred to as The New Earth.

The New Earth will be a reality but it needs to start with you taking full responsibility for your thoughts and actions. You are not your thoughts, however much they convince you that you are. You are the silence outside of your thoughts. You are the stillness that is overridden by all the noise from your mind chatter. You are stillness, you are peace, you are unconditional love, you are wisdom and knowing that how the world is currently run and working is not conducive to a human being.

Any form of negativity is the ego at play – the

mind chatter trying to convince you of its authority over you. But this is an illusion. It will often send you into the future to worry, panic and become anxious about outcomes for you, to find through your experience that what had been projected didn't actually happen. It caused you a huge amount of stress and anxiety for absolutely no reason – just so it could try and convince you that it was in control. But here's the juxtaposition. It was and is a divine instrument for helping you to realise who you are not. Until the time is necessary it is important for you to believe that the mind is in charge – it cannot be any other way. But as you start on the journey of true self-realization so you come to see that the mind was in fact a necessary illusion, but one that you are ready to relinquish if inner peace is your goal, and true sanity and happiness your intention in this lifetime. However it is much easier said than done. When you have been conditioned all of your life to rely on your mind and its thoughts it is a very difficult pattern to come to break, and accept. The phrase 'the truth will set you free' refers to this entirely. It refers to the truth that when you are set free from your mind you have found real freedom. It is not anything outside of yourselves. It is the freedom of knowing who you truly are. The freedom from inner turmoil. The freedom from mind chatter. The freedom to be still within and follow your true self in all its greatness. It is the freedom to be big, without compromising who you are. This freedom brings you unprecedented joy, for you know deep within you,

you are finally honouring who you really are. No feeling can come close to it, that I can tell you.

As you rise in consciousness you realise that the mind has served as a valuable tool but can take you no further. Only complete surrender to the I AM, to the presence within you (often described as your soul) can take you to your next stage of realisation. It's the complete letting go of the past, full acceptance of the present and release of the illusion of the future. Time in enlightened consciousness is now. It is full acceptance of whatever is happening now. It is without judgement, condemnation and negativity – it is what is – it is perfectly occurring in the now in total alignment with your soul. It has always been this way, that life was always about the soul and not the body and mind - it's just that most people's perceptions cannot reach this truth and as a consequence so much suffering occurs, not realising that the soul was in charge all along. Please stop, and re-read the last sentence because it's one of the most important ones in this book. The soul has always been in charge, but without the unwavering reality that you are a soul how can this perception be believed? It can't. It is only on the ladder to real self-realisation that the truth starts to become your reality and this is where the importance of the Pineal Gland comes in. It is the doorway to enlightenment. It works in unison with your heart to activate unconditional love from within you. It is coming to know the real you who only knows how to love - everything else you have been taught how to do.

The purpose of activating your Pineal Gland is to come back to the true you. To realising that you have never been separated from Source, that you are divine wisdom and unconditional love. The labels for this state are not important it's the feeling and knowing the truth that is. Connecting fully back to your divine power starts now!

Helen Jane Rose

Epilogue from The Enlightened Conscious Collaboration...

You who are reading this short but powerful book are the leaders of the New Earth. The New Earth is based around co-operation, compassion and higher consciousness. We wish to ignite in you the fire to worry not about what anyone else thinks of you. To bravely live your truth, your inner moral compass and your soul on your sleeve. The more who are prepared to do this, the quicker the conscious revolution will play out. You are being called to stop playing small. It isn't serving you, or the world. We ask you to step fully into the light that you really are and ask that you start to remember your big, bright purpose for being here. We ask you to stand tall – not small. To stand at the threshold of an evolutionary time that will be talked about in text books in the future on the planet. Many alive today will be remembered as the 'chosen' ones. There will be many. You are at the threshold of great change. It's time to transmute suffering into acceptance, grief and trauma into happiness and joy. We have put forward to you (through this book and the audio activation) a profound step in getting there. Here is the link again to the Pineal Gland

Activation Audio: www.soulconsciousbeing.com/pineal-gland-activation/

Please don't underestimate its importance. It's a stepping stone to fully activating your Pineal Gland. It is Soul Conscious Technology at its best.

CONTACT

Helen Jane Rose is the author of *To Fear, With Love – A Story of Urban Enlightenment* published by Roundfire Books and *Wake Up: Spiritual Enlightenment Uncloaked.* Both books are available on Amazon or through the author's website:
www.soulconsciousbeing.com

You'll also find information about 1-to-1 Soul Alignment Sessions, Frequency Activations & Automatic Writing Mentoring, free audios, activations and audio tools, an open-hearted blog & messages from The Enlightened Conscious Collaboration at
www.soulconsciousbeing.com

To contact the author please send an email to:
info@soulconsciousbeing.com

Made in the USA
Monee, IL
02 June 2021

70035352R00046